3 0738 00149 8756

Presidents Day

Dianne M. MacMillan

Reading Consultant:

Michael P. French, Ph.D.
Bowling Green State University

—Best Holiday Books—

Enslow Publishers, Inc.

40 Industrial Road
Box 398
Berkeley Heights, NJ 07922
USA

PO Box 38
Aldershot
Hants GU12 6BP
UK

http://www.enslow.com

COLUSA COUNTY FREE LIBRARY

Acknowledgments

The author would like to thank Maxine N. Lurie, professor of American history, Seton Hall University, for her careful review of the manuscript.

Copyright © 1997 by Enslow Publishers, Inc.

All rights reserved.

No part of this book may be reproduced by any means without the written permission of the publisher.

Library of Congress Cataloging-in-Publication Data

MacMillan, Dianne.
Presidents Day / Dianne M. MacMillan.
p. cm. — (Best holiday books)
Includes index.
Summary: Provides brief accounts of the lives of two prominent U.S. presidents and describes the holiday that was established in their honor.
ISBN 0-89490-820-0
1. Presidents' Day—Juvenile literature. 2. Washington, George, 1732-1799—Juvenile literature. 3. Lincoln, Abraham, 1809-1865—Juvenile literature. 4. Presidents—United States— Biography—Juvenile literature. [1. Presidents' Day. 2. Washington, George, 1732-1799. 3. Lincoln, Abraham, 1809-1865. 4. Presidents.] I. Title. II. Series.
E176.8.M13 1997
973.4'1'092—dc20
[B]

96-27290
CIP
AC

Printed in the United States of America

10 9 8 7 6 5 4 3 2

Illustration Credits:
© Diane C. Lyell, p. 4; Dianne M. MacMillan, p. 38; Library of Congress, pp. 10, 15, 16, 17, 18, 24, 26, 31; Mrs. Kevin Scheibel, pp. 40, 41; National Park Service, pp. 21, 32, 37; Photo courtesy of the Washington, D.C., Convention and Visitors Association, pp. 8, 36.

Cover Illustration: Mrs. Kevin Scheibel

Contents

In 1789 George Washington became our country's first president.

Two Great Men

On a spring day in 1789, people stood along Cherry Street in New York City and cheered. A tall man rode slowly along in his carriage. Dressed in a brown suit with white silk stockings, the man waved to the crowd. The carriage stopped outside the Federal Hall building on Wall Street. Fifty-seven-year-old George Washington stepped out. This tall—six foot two inch—man with powdered hair would soon be sworn in as our country's first president.

The city celebrated with parades and fireworks. Thirteen cannons were fired. One cannon was fired for each state. George

Washington was a hero. He had led our country through the American Revolution (1775–1783) to win independence from Great Britain. With courage and a sense of fairness he guided our young nation through its first struggling years.

Forty years later a boy living in Indiana read a book over and over. The book was about George Washington. This boy, Abraham Lincoln, grew up to be the sixteenth president of the United States. He, too, led our country through a terrible war—the Civil War (1861–1865). Again, as with Washington, his courage and sense of fairness kept our country from being destroyed.

On the third Monday of February each year, we honor these two great men. Many things about their lives were different. But they shared one thing in common. They both loved our country. Let's find out more about them and why we celebrate Presidents Day.

Young George Washington

George Washington was born on a large farm in Virginia on February 22, 1732. As a boy he swam, sailed in the river, and rode horses on the farm. George liked to spend time with his older half-brother Lawrence, who was a soldier. Lawrence told him about his war experiences.

George's father died when George was eleven years old. This was a very sad time. He helped his mother take care of the farm and his younger brothers and sister.

George's father left most of his property to Lawrence. After a few years George went to live with Lawrence at Mount Vernon, the family estate on the Potomac River. George loved Mount Vernon. He became an expert horse rider. He learned how to shoot a gun, dance, and play cards. The life of a Virginia gentleman was very pleasant. Lawrence was like a second father to George.

George was good in math and learned how to

Mount Vernon was the Washington family estate on the Potomac River.

use surveyor's tools. A surveyor measures and marks the boundaries of land. At age sixteen he spent a month surveying thousands of acres of land. That land belonged to the family of his neighbor, Colonel William Fairfax. George loved camping in the wilderness and riding his horse.

That happiness changed to sadness four years later when Lawrence died of a lung disease. George was filled with sorrow. Mount Vernon now belonged to him. With a heavy heart he followed in Lawrence's footsteps by becoming a Virginia volunteer soldier. His first orders were to deliver a warning to French soldiers camped by the Ohio River in territory claimed by Great Britain. The trip took forty days and covered a distance of over one thousand miles.

Fighting broke out between French and British soldiers in 1754. This was the start of the French and Indian War. Washington became the commander of Virginia's solders at age twenty-three. After seven years Great Britain won the war. It had gained all the territory east of the Mississippi River as well as Canada. George

George Washington and Martha Dandridge Custis were married on January 6, 1759.

Washington was now an experienced soldier. News of his bravery and courage spread through the colonies.

Washington returned to Mount Vernon. In 1759 he married Martha Dandridge Custis. She was a widow with two small children. She was also one of the richest women in America. With Martha's money, Washington began buying many of the nearby farms surrounding Mount Vernon. He planned to spend the rest of his life as a farmer. But events changed Washington's plans.

George Washington Leads Our Country

After the French and Indian War, Great Britain needed to raise money to pay war debts. King George put a tax on the paper, tea, and paint that the colonists bought. This angered many of the colonists. They thought that the king was unfair and refused to pay the taxes.

In 1774 representatives from each colony met in Philadelphia, Pennsylvania. The purpose of the meeting was to decide what to do about the policies of Great Britain. They called their meeting the Continental Congress. George

Washington was a representative from Virginia. He did not like to speak in public to large groups. Still he was an excellent listener and very fair. Other members of the congress valued his opinion. Patrick Henry, a representative from Virginia, said that Washington was able to make decisions better than anyone else. The representatives finally decided that, if necessary, they would unite and meet the British with force.

On April 19, 1775, British troops fired on colonists in Lexington, Massachusetts. Eight Americans were killed and ten were wounded. As word of the battle spread, Americans were shocked and angry. They were ready to fight the British.

A Second Continental Congress was called. Someone would have to lead the American soldiers against the British. George Washington was everyone's choice. Washington thought that he was not qualified, but he agreed to do his best. He refused to take any pay except expenses. Washington went straight from the meeting in Philadelphia to take command of the troops.

For the next eight years General Washington trained and led the American soldiers. At first the Americans were successful. They drove the British out of Boston. But as time went on the American army grew smaller and weaker. Sometimes there was not enough food or weapons. The winter weather was bitter cold. At Valley Forge, Pennsylvania, where the troops camped for the winter of 1777–1778, some of the men did not have shoes. In spite of the hardship and lack of supplies, General Washington encouraged his men to keep fighting.

The Americans lost many battles. Yet General Washington would not give up. Many times he surprised the British by attacking when they least suspected it. At the Battle of Trenton, he had his army row across the Delaware River on Christmas Eve. At dawn on Christmas Day the Americans surrounded the enemy troops.

Finally, in 1781, the British general Lord Cornwallis surrendered to Washington at Yorktown, Virginia. The battles of the American Revolution were over.

Washington went home to Mount Vernon. He was tired and ready for a long rest. The farm needed work. It had been neglected all the years he was away fighting. But again his country called him. America needed a new government and new laws to guide it.

Representatives from each state met in 1787 to decide on the new laws and government.

The winter at Valley Forge, Pennsylvania, was very harsh and some of the men did not have shoes.

George Washington was one representative of Virginia. He was also elected president of the Constitutional Convention.

In this new government a president would be elected by the people. George Washington was the unanimous choice. But Washington was worried. He was a soldier and a landowner. Could he run a country? George Washington was

Lord Cornwallis surrendered to George Washington after the Battle of Yorktown, Virginia.

On April 30, 1789, George Washington was sworn in as the first president of the United States.

afraid. This man of great courage in battle did not want to disappoint the people that believed in him.

On April 30, 1789, George Washington became president of the United States. He did not want to be a king. He understood that whatever he did would be an example for future presidents. Four years later he was elected to

George Washington spent his retirement years tending crops and entertaining visitors.

another term. Under his leadership our young democracy became stronger.

After serving two terms he returned to Mount Vernon. He spent his retirement tending crops and entertaining visitors. Two years later Washington developed a bad cold. Doctors tried everything to help him recover. He died two days later on December 14, 1799, at the age of sixty-seven. He had served his country for most of his life. He was buried at Mount Vernon. All praised him as the "Father of Our Country."

Abraham Lincoln

On February 12, 1809, Abraham Lincoln was born in a log cabin in Kentucky. Because his family was poor, Abraham's life was very different from George Washington's. But like George Washington, Abraham lost a parent when he was young. His father, Thomas, moved the family to Indiana when Abraham was seven. Two years later, his mother Nancy died.

Abraham grew tall and strong. He helped his father clear the land. His eleven-year-old sister Sarah tried to do the cooking and cleaning. But it was too much for her. Thomas Lincoln decided to remarry. His new wife's name was Sarah Bush

Johnston. Abraham and Sarah liked their new stepmother.

Everyone on the farm had to work. There was no regular school. Sometimes a teacher traveling through the area would agree to teach for a few weeks in exchange for food. All of Abraham's and Sarah's schooling added up to only a few months.

Yet that did not stop Abraham from reading.

Abraham Lincoln was born in a log cabin similar to this one on February 12, 1809.

He loved books, and he read over and over the few books that he owned. Abraham borrowed books from friends and neighbors. His cousin Dennis Hanks said, "I never saw Abe after he was twelve that he didn't have a book in his hand or in his pocket." Abraham read about George Washington and he read Defoe's book *Robinson Crusoe*. *Aesop's Fables* was another of his favorites. He also read the Bible.

Abraham loved to sit and listen to the old men tell stories. After awhile he joined the storytelling. As he grew older he walked miles to listen to a preacher or to a visiting lawyer who was arguing a case in court. Afterwards Abraham would copy the way the speaker talked and moved, bringing laughter to his listeners.

When Lincoln was nineteen a man hired him to sail a cargo boat down the Mississippi River to New Orleans. It was an exciting trip. New Orleans was the largest city that Lincoln had ever seen. There was so much to see and do. Then he saw something he would never forget. African-American men, women, and children were chained together. As he watched, slave dealers sold the people like cattle.

Lincoln returned home. In 1830 his father moved the family to a new farm in Illinois. Lincoln chopped trees and helped build a new cabin.

One year later Lincoln left the farm. He moved to the small town of New Salem, Illinois. There he worked in a store and later ran the town's post office. The schoolmaster became his friend and loaned him books to read. Lincoln also read the newspapers that came into the post office. He learned what was happening in other parts of Illinois and in the government.

After a year the store he worked in closed. However, Lincoln and a partner, William Berry, opened another store. Lincoln enjoyed his new life. But his partner died suddenly and left him with a lot of bills. To pay the debts, Lincoln taught himself how to survey land. He worked as a surveyor just as George Washington had done. As he traveled around the area people got to know him. They enjoyed talking to Lincoln and listening to his stories. At night he studied law.

In 1830, Abraham Lincoln chopped trees and helped his father build a new cabin.

Lincoln enjoyed public speaking. He thought that politics would be a good career for him. In 1834 he won a seat in the Illinois general assembly. He moved to the state capital in Vandalia. Two years later he was re-elected. He served three terms.

When Springfield became the new capital in 1837, Lincoln moved again. He had passed the exam to become a lawyer in 1836. When the assembly was not in session he practiced law.

In 1842 Lincoln married Mary Ann Todd. Mary came from a wealthy family. Her family was against the marriage. The family thought that Lincoln would not amount to anything. Lincoln became a successful lawyer. Mary and Abraham lived in a big house in Springfield and had four sons.

Lincoln was elected to the United States House of Representatives in 1846. The Lincoln family moved to Washington, D.C. Lincoln left the House after one term in office. Still he kept speaking about problems that he thought were important. Slavery was one of those problems.

Abraham Lincoln and Mary Todd Lincoln had four sons, two of whom are seen here.

In 1858 he ran for the United States Senate. His opponent was Stephen A. Douglas. The two candidates could not have looked more different. Lincoln was six feet four inches tall. He towered over Douglas who was barely five feet four inches tall. They held several debates. Thousands of people turned out to hear them speak.

The question of slavery was dividing the country. Southerners depended on slaves to work on the plantations. Many people in the North said that slavery was wrong. Lincoln agreed with the northerners. He hoped that the practice of slavery would either die or stop by itself. He was worried that the slavery problem would destroy the country. In one of his speeches he said, "A house divided against itself cannot stand. I believe this government cannot endure permanently half slavc and half free."

Newspaper reporters wrote about Lincoln. When the votes were counted, Douglas won by a narrow margin. Lincoln was disappointed. However, people all over the country now knew who Abraham Lincoln was.

Lincoln Becomes Our Sixteenth President

In 1860 the Republican party chose Lincoln as its candidate for president. The Republicans were against the expansion of slavery.

The Democratic party was divided. They chose two candidates. Stephen A. Douglas represented the North, and John Breckinridge represented the South. Lincoln received the most electoral votes and was elected the sixteenth president of the United States.

Many people in the South did not want a president who was against slavery. The state of

South Carolina seceded (or left) the Union. A month later six other southern states also seceded. Later four more states joined the others. These states formed their own country. They called themselves the Confederate States of America, or the Confederacy.

In 1861 southern soldiers attacked United States troops at Fort Sumter, South Carolina. This action began the Civil War. For the next four years Union soldiers from the North and Confederate soldiers from the South fought many battles.

Hundreds of thousands of men died. Often the soldiers were young boys. It was not unusual for boys fifteen or younger to join the military. Abraham Lincoln did not want war. On the other hand he did not want the United States to destroy itself.

Many people wondered about Lincoln's ability to lead the nation. Some were unhappy with his decisions. Many wanted him to stop the war. Every day he received angry letters. Still

Lincoln refused to change his mind. He felt strongly that he had to keep the country together.

In the summer of 1862 he called his cabinet members into his office. The cabinet members were men chosen to advise him. He read to them a paper called the Emancipation Proclamation. This document stated that the slaves would become free when the North won the war.

In July 1863 a terrible, bloody battle took place at Gettysburg, Pennsylvania. After three days of fighting, more than fifty thousand Union and Confederate soldiers lay dead on the battlefield.

A few months later people wanted to honor the many dead soldiers. They held a special ceremony at Gettysburg. Many important people gathered to listen to Edward Everett of Massachusetts, the main speaker. Everett spoke for two hours. Then President Lincoln stood to say a few words. He began, "Fourscore and seven years ago our fathers brought forth on this continent, a new nation . . ." The speech was short. It took less than three minutes to give. Still it became Lincoln's most famous speech. Today the words are often quoted whenever Lincoln or the Civil War is remembered. Abraham Lincoln was one of the greatest speakers of all our country's presidents.

In 1865, almost two years after Gettysburg, Confederate General Robert E. Lee surrendered

The bloodiest battle of the Civil War was fought near Gettysburg, Pennsylvania, in 1863.

A national cemetery honors the many soldiers that died in the Battle of Gettysburg.

to Union General Ulysses S. Grant in Virginia. The Civil War was over. It was the bloodiest American war. More than six hundred thousand Union and Confederate soldiers died. The nation was whole again. Lincoln looked forward to rebuilding our country.

Five days later Lincoln and his wife went to Ford's Theater to watch a play. During the third act Lincoln was shot by an actor named John Wilkes Booth. Lincoln died the next morning on April 15, 1865, at the age of fifty-seven.

Secretary of War Edwin M. Stanton said, “Now he belongs to the ages.” The country mourned the loss of this fair and honest man. Confederate General Robert E. Lee said, “The South has lost its best friend.”

Honoring Our Two Greatest Presidents

Americans celebrated George Washington's birthday years before his death. His troops celebrated at Valley Forge. During each year of his presidency his birthday was a joyous occasion with balls and parties. In the 1800s his birthday became a legal holiday throughout our country.

On February 12, 1892, Lincoln's birthday became a legal holiday in Illinois. Thirty-two northern states followed Illinois's example. There are many ways in which our country honors these two great presidents.

Streets, squares, cities, and schools are named after them. Washington also has a state named after him and our nation's capital. Thirty-two states have Washington counties. And there are over one hundred post office branches named for our first president.

In our nation's capital there are two great memorials that millions of people visit each year. The Washington Monument is an obelisk (a tall, tapering, four-sided pillar) over five hundred and fifty feet high. The Lincoln Memorial is built like a Greek temple. Inside is a nineteen-foot statue of Lincoln.

The $1 bill has a picture of George Washington, and the $5 bill has a picture of Abraham Lincoln. Quarters and pennies also show their faces. On Mount Rushmore in South Dakota, the heads of Washington and Lincoln are carved in a granite cliff, along with the heads of two other presidents, Thomas Jefferson and Theodore Roosevelt.

In 1971 Congress set the third Monday in February as a special day to remember the

The Washington Monument in Washington, D.C., towers over five hundred and fifty feet high.

Father of Our Country. In recent years Abraham Lincoln has also been honored on the third Monday of February. The day is called Presidents Day.

On Mount Rushmore National Monument in the Black Hills of South Dakota, the heads of George Washington and Abraham Lincoln are carved in the cliff, along with two other presidents, Thomas Jefferson and Theodore Roosevelt.

Schools and federal offices are closed on Presidents Day and many homes fly the American flag.

Presidents Day

Schools and federal offices are closed on Presidents Day. There is no mail delivery. During the month of February boys and girls learn about the lives of these two great men. Bulletin boards in classrooms show the presidents' pictures and some of the events in their lives. Children read books about both of them. More books have been written about Abraham Lincoln than any other American.

In some schools children act out plays about Washington and the American Revolution, and about Lincoln and the Civil War. Many read and

During the month of February boys and girls learn about the lives of George Washington and Abraham Lincoln.

memorize some of the presidents' speeches and famous words.

At Mount Vernon there is a wreath-laying ceremony at George Washington's grave. In Hodgenville, Kentucky, a wreath is placed at the

Presidents Day is a celebration for all Americans.

door of the cabin where Lincoln was born. Another wreath is placed in front of the Lincoln statue at the Lincoln Memorial. Then the Gettysburg Address is read aloud.

At Gettysburg, Springfield, Valley Forge, and Yorktown, people remember how these two men changed the course of our country. Both men loved freedom and justice. And both men stood up for what they believed. Presidents Day is a celebration for all Americans. Happy Birthday, George Washington! Happy Birthday, Abraham Lincoln!

Note to Parents, Teachers, and Librarians

We are aware that some publications choose to punctuate the holiday "Presidents Day" with an apostrophe after the *s*. However, we have chosen to follow Associated Press-style throughout this book, and have thus foregone the apostrophe.

Glossary

cabinet—A group of people chosen to advise the President.

candidate—A person who seeks to be elected to an office.

Confederacy—The eleven southern states that tried to leave the Union.

congress—A group of people who make laws.

Continental Congress—A group of men from each colony who met together twice to plan America's opposition to the policies of Great Britain.

debate—To talk or discuss at a public meeting.

Democratic party—One of the two main political parties of the United States.

emancipate—To set free from slavery or control.

obelisk—A tall, tapering, four-sided pillar ending in a small pyramid.

plantation—A large farm.

politics—The profession of holding public office.

Republican party—One of the two main political parties of the United States.

representative—A person chosen to speak or act for others.

secede—To withdraw from a group or organization.

survey—To measure land to find its boundaries and size.

surveyor—Someone whose work is surveying land.

term—A definite period of time, related to holding office.

Union—The United States of America.

Index